Drowning in the Floating World

Drowning
in the
Floating World

ADVANCE READING COPY
for review purposes only

Poems

Meg Eden

Press 53
Winston-Salem

Press 53, LLC
PO Box 30314
Winston-Salem, NC 27130

First Edition

IMMERSION POETRY SERIES
edited by Christopher Forrest

Cover Art by Ogata Gekkō (1859–1920)

Author Photo by Meg Eden

Cover design by Kevin Morgan Watson and Christopher Forrest

Library of Congress Control Number
2019951167

ADVANCE READING COPY
for review purposes only

Printed on acid-free paper
ISBN 978-1-950413-15-7

Many thanks to the editors of the following journals, where versions of these poems first appeared:

Blotterature, "In Tokyo, three months after the earthquake"

carte blanche, "I Ask My Mother What It's Like, Living at the Bottom of the Ocean" and "Coming Home after a Tsunami"

Cha: An Asian Literary Journal, "Burusera"

Commonweal, "Okinawa Aquarium"

Contemporary Verse 2, "A String of Buoys Arrive on Oahu Beach," "Poem for the Sneakers Washing Onshore," "mizuko," "Things to Do in My Hometown: Higashimatsushima," "okada" and "Ningyo Kuyo (Doll Funeral Ceremony)"

Cresset, "Baptism"

drafthorse, "Corpse Washing"

Gargoyle, "Tokyo Steakhouse"

Hawaii Review, "Rumiko / A Series of Possessions," "Radium Girls"

Kitaab, "The Water Trade"

Matter Press, "Looking at an Abandoned Russian Theme Park in Niigata, Japan"

Rattle, "Tohoku Ghost Stories"

Tinderbox Poetry Journal, "All Summer I Wore"

ZO magazine, "Hokotashi City, Ibaraki Prefecture"

"Burusera" was listed as a finalist for the Cha "Addiction" Poetry Contest

"Rumiko / A Series of Possessions" won the 2015 Ian MacMillan Award in Poetry

"Radium Girls" won the 2015 Ian MacMillan Award in Poetry

"The Water Trade" was included in "The Best of Kitaab, 2018"

"Hokotashi City, Ibaraki Prefecture" was reprinted in *Nostrovia!*

Contents

*

*Oh that my monks robe
were wide enough
to gather up all
the suffering people
in this floating world*

—Ryōkan

Drowning in the Floating World

Hokotashi City, Ibaraki Prefecture

*Six days before the massive magnitude-9 earthquake that triggered
the devastating March 11, 2011 tsunami in northeastern Japan,
50 melon-headed whales beached themselves in the area. This
week, over 150 melon-headed whales beached themselves on
two beaches in the same vicinity.*
—Paul Seaburn, *Mysterious Universe*, April 14th 2015

The day is gray with a beach
covered in whales. Sand

becomes water and water
an uninhabitable place.

People still surf but how can they ignore
the fifty bodies, like tea leaves

at the bottom of a scryer's glass,
heavy and loud in memorial?

The Coast Guard carries water
to pour over the bodies.

What do they expect? That the dolphins
will walk back to the ocean?

So many put down. So many
already dead—one by one,

scooped up by the bulldozer
and returned to the ocean.

Can anyone know what will happen
six days from now? Six hours?

On the shore, one body flails against
the others, craving the water

that pulls—both killing
and sustaining.

Onagawa

the steady siren from a shipyard port

exodus, brown water—dry land!

evacuation broadcasts echo through an empty street

the sound of water rising up a wall

     & silence

the road, a growing crowd of living trash

that bridge once felt so high above the ground

the street is now a charcoal river snake

a house floats down the street the way

     a toy bobs in a bath—

is there a girl still sitting in that house

a truck between a shop & house:

     the three become one flesh

our street is now a hungry ocean mouth

there—a house rehearses catching fire!

sitting on a roof someone records it all, while crying:

     nande-yo nande-yo nande-yo

& all the while the snow & the

     snow & the snow

That First Night, the Hospital

was the only thing left standing.
Those of us who got to it in time
sat on the third floor, praying. Thank God
for generators, why God, the generators—
that, unharmed, kept the lights on,
the only lights in our city? Outside,
Atlantis formed—my house
somewhere underneath us.
Over the dark, people floated, crying
for help, crying as if there was any way
we could get them out of the water,
as if there was any room here.
Someone shut the curtains. Even so,
we heard them until morning.

Things to Do in My Hometown: Higashimatsushima

after Gary Snyder

Become a spirit & wander as a lantern
through a nostalgic alleyway.
Thrift shop in the ruins of a mall.
Make miso out of seaweed from a backyard,
make udon from the debris in a living room.
Try to remember friends' names, & what
they looked like before they were found.
Watch the water recede.
Watch someone at the top of the hill
build what looks like a shed for a dog.
Imagine living in a dog's house, imagine being
a dog living in a neighbor's house.
Make a list of places to move to. Go through the house
& find what has & has not been affected.
(Is the milk still good? The nattô?) Make a map
of where all the buildings used to be. Go to the woods
to find something living. Go find a fox,
ask how many tails it takes to outsmart disaster.
Tell the fox what it means
to be a survivor, & watch the fox
tend to its young. Think about what it's like
to be the tsunami: filling the earth,
subduing it: to be fruitful & multiply, multiply, multiply,
dominion over fish, birds
and over every living thing that moves about the earth.

Town Hall

Watching the town resurrect,
I remain unfixed,
mouth filled with birds.

My eyes are dusty & split
down the middle; my bowels
washed in mud. A car

rests in my intestines.
The dog in my chest
just delivered puppies.

I've been given many names:
Dangerous, あぶない。
Do not enter, 入ってはいけません。

Tsunami, you may have
erased my neighbors,
but still I remain!

I defy you, Tsunami.
I defy you, Town.
I will always remember

should you mistakenly
forget. Here I stand,
a new tsunami stone.

Rumiko / A Series of Possessions

*Over the course of last summer, Reverend Kaneda exorcised
25 spirits from Rumiko Takahashi. . . . 'All the people who
came,' Kaneda said, 'and each one of the stories they told had
some connection with water.'*
—Ghosts of the Tsunami, Richard Lloyd Parry

I.

Yesterday I became a dog:
I didn't want to, but it
was barking so loudly
I couldn't bear it.
Making rice, I opened
the door of my body,
and that starving dog ate—
three men had to hold
me down as it entered.

*It's been three years
since I last ate*, the dog said—
assuming I can translate
the dog, that the dog thinks
in years, that the dog feels
something like loneliness
from that couple who forgot
to unchain him when they left.

I understood that smell
from the local power plant,
in time, overbearing. And the silence
that followed. And the emaciated
dog that followed the silence.

II.

My wife lives in one
of the temporary metal huts
on top of the mountain.

After all this time,
no one has given her a real home.
Does anyone think about the old
besides the old?
She has a shoebox where she keeps
a white rope and strokes it occasionally.
I watch her, worrying
what she might do.

III.

—when I reached the side
of the mountain, I still thought
it was good to be alive.

I looked down at our city,
which spun like dirty laundry—

and realized that there must be
many dead people today, prayed
that I didn't know any of them,

but when my two daughters
were not found, I sought them
in a different place—

Still, I wander heaven
and haven't found them.
Have you seen my daughters?

IV.

Every time
I wake from war, I wake up
wet with seawater.

It's like how, as a girl,
I'd get up from my chair
to a ring of blood
dripping from me, always following.
A thousand spirits wrestle me,
pressing, trying to get inside
as if I'm a place of pilgrimage.
But what about me tastes so good?
When will I find rest?

V.

Okaa-san! Okaa-san!
The girl inside me cries.
Sometimes, she is so young
that all she knows to do is cry.
Other times she apologizes
for letting go of her brother
in that always-coming
big black wave—

The priest's wife must grab
my hand and say, *Mummy's
here. Let's go together.*
Eventually, the girl says,
I can go on my own now.
You can let go of me.

I let go and wake up
relieved, my body light.
I remember who I am:
a woman about to be married.

VI.

Each person had eight minutes.

I don't know what Kaori was doing,
probably in a classroom somewhere
with all those children and that water—
there must've been a lot of pushing.

But what did it matter in the end?
There were boats on top of buildings,
now, so many other parents looking
through piles of debris for a familiar jacket,
a lunch box, a haircut.

How do I tell Kaori's father
about the twenty thousand bodies
at the bottom of the ocean,
his daughter perpetually dying
inside my mouth?

I was not there, but sometimes
I see it in dreams: far away, the water.

mizuko

potential buddha is
aborted buddha is
buried buddha

*

wading in a life/death river
death the washing machine
recycles bodies into water

*

someone comes by
and gives all the stone fetuses
red hats for winter

*

a daughter buries herself in her mother
the mother buries her under the house
the water buries the daughter in a new body

*

the mother drinks from the daughter
the mother is buried inside the daughter
the mother and daughter inhabit the same body

*

every fall a mother apologizes
gifts for her stone daughter
another molding doll

Rikuzentakata

A year after the tsunami,
a fifty-year-old son
digs with his hands
through the mud
for his mother.

Maybe her shoes?
A familiar pattern from her dress?
Everyone digs for someone
but nobody finds
who they're looking for—

Outside the town hall, a lost
& found for the dead: shopping
baskets filled with photo albums
& a wall lined with children's red
backpacks, still full.

Corpse Washing

after Rilke

I've grown used to all the bodies.
But when the light reveals
what's missing of her, I realize
that working with the dead
doesn't make them any less strange.

Her family shows me her class
picture, I compare it to
the body in front of me:
bones shaped like a hand; a burrow
of dark wet flesh, overrun by maggots.

I wash what remains of her
under the funeral garb and, knowing
nothing of drowning, everything
of drowning, I imagine
the journey of her body.

I patch in the maggot holes. I fill
her mouth with cotton. The mother
brings me the lipstick she used to wear—
a bubblegum pink—and for a moment,
the girl's lips look soft and alive.

I brush the seaweed and trash
from her remaining hair until it's soft.
I clip the ends of my hair to fill
her empty eyebrows, her missing eyelashes.
In front, the mother weeps, loud

like a wave, all the while the father
looks ahead, still. The girl on the table,
also still. Only the young boy squirms
and clears his throat. Unable to look
at his sister, his eyes wander

over the tatami floor to the screen
door that, against the light
outside reflects the shadow
of a stranger: a peach tree
contorted and brittle like

the girl's hand, which I try to pose
into a symbol of prayer. The beads
between her fingers cannot hide
the skeletal hand, a ghost
against the fleshy one.

The mother takes
the last water to her daughter's
lips, but the girl rejects it.
She's had more than enough
water for one life.

This is how we say farewell:
the girl's favorite dress is brought.
A summer dress, short sleeved
and red like poppies. Laid over
her body, the dress is engulfing.

Inside her coffin, the girl is lifted
to the oven. The fire is living and god-like.
She is fed into it, quickly,
before anyone can imagine her burning-alive
hair, the gnashing of that poppy dress.

Tsunami Girl

after Bertolt Brecht's "About a Drowned Girl"

Once the water ate her & she propelled
through the streets into buildings
& alleyways, a Fox's Wedding shone
through the rain as if patting her back
in polite consolation.

Seaweed & debris took the body
with them. A book swam
against her leg; chairs & telephone poles
interrupted, making even
this last journey relentless.

The evening sky became dark with smoke,
& at night, the stars were hesitant.
But as it got early, the sky
lit, confident like a lantern.
So the world continued around her.

It happened quite slowly: her pale flesh rotted,
slipping from nature, from her family's thoughts.
First, her face, then hands, and only at the very end,
her hair. Only then was she counted
collateral in a city filled with collateral.

All Summer I Wore

dead girls' dresses.
I wore dresses I found on the shore, in now-empty homes.
I wore the sun.
I wore the muddy water that carried my neighbors' bodies.
I wore the boat that rose up to become a mountain.
I wore the bodies of beached dolphins.
I wore washed-up Chinese newspapers & Russian bottles.
I wore melon crates.
I wore a government hand-out blanket.
I wore the unclaimed backpack of an elementary school boy.
I wore my great grandmother's lost tablet.
I wore the names of my classmates, etched in my arm.
I wore altars to washed-away gods.
I wore a uniform from another city.
I wore the laws of my father.
I wore the smile girls are expected to wear.
I wore the dead girls whose dresses I stole.
I wore the kappa who reaches out of the lake, trying to pull me under.
I wore a new gospel as my shoes.
I wore driftwood
& got dressed for the ocean.

I Ask My Mother What It's Like, Living at the Bottom of the Ocean.

She says, *yes—it's a bit dark*
and cold, but you can get used
to anything with time.

I imagine my mother: setting up doilies
on eel cave rocks, polishing
a coral reef. Already, she's probably

cleaned half the disaster debris
from the ocean floor.
It must be beautiful, I say—*what*

with all those fish down there.
You have all the unagi-don you could ever
want now, right? I laugh.

My mother gets harder to see.
You must be busy, she says.
I'll join you soon, I joke.

My mother says nothing.
My mother reaches out to give me
a gift but her hands are empty.

She keeps gesturing toward me,
her translucent hands
like two fish. I ask her what

she is trying to give me.
And then I see it—my two hands
against hers, how full and pink.

okada

months after the earthquake / inside the exclusion zone / the
water has hardened to mud / there are bodies still / there is a
man in white pants & a white jacket / face-down in the mud /
he's suspended like those figures that come inside soap bars /
like someone bobbing for apples with their body / it looks
funny at first until you realize it's a real person / that someone
is probably still looking for this person / they say they've cleaned
all the bodies / off the road / this man is just a few yards away
/ from a distance he blends into the mud / it looks like he could
get up but he doesn't / a city buried inside & under him

Tohoku Ghost Stories

*We remembered the old ghost stories, and we told one
another that there would be many new stories like that.
Personally, I don't believe in the existence of spirits, but
that's not the point. If people say they see ghosts, then
that's fine—we can leave it at that.*
                              —Masashi Hijikata

the old woman who visits me for tea is dead but I don't have the
heart to tell her

every time I see my mother there's a pool of seawater in her room

and still no one's removed that boat off the Sumitomo's building

if a boat can get all the way up there what keeps us from
disappearing into the sky

like the woman who walks each morning across the ocean and
back I wonder where I'm going now

what can I talk to my friend about these days I still *have* my son

who collects the things found on the beach someone's television
set a rusted refrigerator

a woman says that soon this city will be filled by God but is God
a tsunami that takes years to drain out

the phone calls I get are from numbers that don't exist

my husband calls his friends several times a day *how are you?
how are you?* just in case

Otsuchi becomes a great washing machine again tumbling us in
and out of memories

it's come to the point I can't even go out in the rain anymore that's
when I see

puddles like the eyes of dead people what can I do put them in a cup

my daughters were lined up like bowling pins outside the school
waiting for the earthquake

why didn't I keep her home from school that day she complained about her throat

every day someone new is sick whatever we try to rebuild is barricaded by ghosts

even taxi drivers refuse to go to Sendai afraid of catching ghosts

one man's address led to a concrete slab the man was gone but the driver opened the door

just in case I was never high enough I kept climbing the stairs but how do you outrun an ocean

with all the old houses cleared and the new ones rising it's becoming hard to remember what we looked like before

NASA Satellite Triolet

Whatever happened to the beach?
Did it float away into the sea?
Or is it buried somewhere, asleep?
Whatever happened to the beach
can't be undone. The blue reach
fills the pockets of Ishinomaki.
Whatever happened to the beach
has floated away into the sea,
capping the bay with floating debris.

Coming Home after a Tsunami

after Shuntaro Tanikawa

Every day I go to my house
where the dishes are covered in seaweed
& the windows are brown with salt.
My mother is dead, my father
is dead, & my dog is emaciated:
tied to a pole, dried out like a fruit skin.
In the wind, he moves like a flag.

Every morning, my house burns down,
& every night it floods. Who have we lost
today—Ichiro? Tatsuki? At some point,
I'll forget the names of the living. I never
see them, only memorials for the dead.
If I had tablets for them all
my house would be a constant funeral.

Some days I wake up inside a whirlpool
of boats & houses & trees—
my missing sister is there too:
spinning, her small mouth open
with fish popping in & out.

At night I dream about empty parking lots:
flat & void of memory.
It's been two years & I still live
in a temporary house. My town is made of
forgotten trash & donated blankets.

Before our town, there is a wall
built by the government, painted
with fish bodies & a portrait of my sister.
Behind the wall, we are forgotten
because there is no one who has to see us.

Poem for the Sneakers Washing Onshore

We're expecting 100 sneakers with bones in them.
—Curt Ebbesmeyer, May 21, 2012

we are the feet of salarymen
& the feet of school girls
& the feet of tennis players
& the feet of arcade gamers
& the feet of stay-at-home moms
& the feet of parasite daughters
& the feet of hikkikomori sons
& the feet of principals
& the feet of janitors
& the feet of Christians
& the feet of Shintos
& the feet of monks
& the feet of porn stars
& the feet of homeless men
& the feet of cross-dressers
& the feet of corpse dressers
& the feet of cartoon otaku
& the feet of old men
& the feet of farmers
& the feet of ganguro girls
& the feet of scarecrows
& the feet of
& the feet of

Villanelle from an Okawa School Mother

I found my daughter
in the middle of the ocean.
Even without her head, I knew her.

When they stopped looking for her,
I had to rent a backhoe. Then,
I found my daughter:

an island for seagulls. If I were
faster, there might have been more left.
Even without her head, I knew her

from that distance. I was sure—
mothers *know*. When
I found my daughter,

I made her bed. She crumbled
once we pulled her from the ocean.
Even without her head, I need her.

She carries inside her a body of water.
No one should forget this. So,
I keep my daughter.
Even without her head, I know her.

Kitsunebi

Kitsune, Japanese fox spirits, are deceivers known on occasion to disguise as humans. Illusory lights are attributed to their magic, known as kitsunebi, or "fox fire."

A woman holds a lantern
over the ocean—we all know
who she is. She is our mother,
the tablet of our grandmother
left behind in the sink in our rush,
the daughter forever studying
for the same exam, a distant
aunt, the girl who is always crying
in public bathrooms.
We all know her but pray
that she'll return to the ocean soon,
that her lantern will dim
before anyone might follow her
out into the cold waves,
that she—that we—might find
peace and, one day, home.

Ningyo Kuyo (Doll Funeral Ceremony)

It takes a hundred years to gain a soul.
      My body, electric & modern, can't become a god—

Attachment gods are made from tears in paper
      lanterns, tired sandal straps, the "well-loved" things.

I was born in a box-womb, I have no memory
      of being formed, of someone placing spirits in my eyes—

The straw of my body molds. Gradually, it expands,
      making me at once both full & hungry.

The room is wet & no one's come to dry me.
      What use is someone's doll in a tsunami?

Once the water's receded, corpses
      are shuttled from our ocean of a town.

The worst fate for any body: to be left
      without a home. If only someone would take

a moment to burn me! Hanabi body, sinking
      ship of me, I cannot bear the entropy

of an abandoned house, my dead owner
      who has outgrown her need for toys.

A fire is brief—it eats & can be satisfied.
      My hunger is ghost-like, it sits like a worm

in my mouth, waiting for burial rites to give it
      a name & to say well done, good & faithful servant.

A Poem by Fukushima Daiichi

I am good-fortune island,
my name means first, best.
I am Tokyo's food,
I am the core of a planet.
I am a burned offering
to myself and my aroma
is pleasing.
I give Japan its name—
I *am* the rising sun.
I am a radioactive god,
I am Titanic.
I do not need testing.
I am a planner—I have
back-up plans for my back-up plans.
I am an abundant hive of villages;
my children won't go hungry.
My children won't be afraid
of waves or shaking floors.
I am TEPCO,
I am government-approved.
I have built my walls up to heaven
and will continue to burn righteous,
my stomach always full, always filling.

Google Reviews of Fukushima Daiichi Power Plant

A Found Poem

Permanently Closed. 3.1 / 5 stars. Sorted by: Most Helpful

10/10 no wait or lines
I saw a fish with five eyes
The people very kind
If you tip them they won't eat you
I feel a deep sadness
No one's ever at the beach, so you can play all alone!
Bring plenty of water or else you'll feel like you're melting down
Makes great electricity
Upgrade recommended
You have killed us all
LOL. I can't believe that google directed me to write a review
    about this place
it was scary, in a good way
Absolutely astonishing, and I got a tumor for FREE
Doing the best they can
The flower will bloom, and bring light to the east Japan
Total bummer
On the plane ride home, I developed an extra eye
amazing but it sad to see the Japanese people die
I would recommend this place for vacations and also for tourist tours
Free anal bleeching onsite
KAWAII NUCREAR DISASSTER!!!!
Hello Fukushima! Tell me how You're doing!?

Fukushima Syndrome

13 March 11

Where have our owners gone?
Every morning, they used to give us water.
Yesterday, I saw them fill their car with bags
and go, but they haven't returned.
When will they return?

Inside me, a storm rises.
Everybody feels it. We all stamp
in our stalls and snort and bellow.
The storm moves wildly inside us.
We feel something different in the air
even though the sun looks the same,
the plants taste the same.
There is a new silence we can't explain.

24 March 11

While everyone else is thinking about
the radiation, I think about my cattle.
I haven't been there to feed them.
Are they still alive right now?
What are they eating?
I go to the temple to pray for my cows.
I tell myself this will be over soon,
that I'll return to feed them the way I did
just a few weeks ago. Who am I kidding?
Some people are saying we won't be able
to return for forty years.
Those were my father's cattle.
When I think of those cattle starving,
I see my father starving.

2 April 11

We are dried up.
Our gates are rusting.
One girl gave birth to a calf
who keeps sucking on a rope
hoping milk will come out.
The calf was born inside drought.
When it was born, we lapped up the blood
its mother gave. The calf can't know

the days we were flooded
with water. What we would give
for a flood! Our friends have died,
we have no choice but to eat their bodies
for the little wetness left inside them.

Our owners are not coming back.
From our stalls, we can see the world
they've built fall apart:
the grass has grown tall,
the building doors swing open.
If only we could celebrate
their ruin from the expanse
of an empty field!

8 May 11

Some of us have returned to our farms.
Many of our cattle are dead.
What little we find alive, we're told
should be destroyed. And what can we do?
Who will eat a radioactive burger?
Or nuclear milk? What is left for us here?
Some of us who can't bear the idea
open the gates and let our cows free.
Look at our livelihood:
a post-apocalyptic street, filled
with wandering cattle.

7 October 11

The silence of an empty barn. A bird
somewhere calls for family.

25 December 11

A farmer returns to his barn
to find the remains of his livestock
mummified: on top of each other,
they create a spider web of bones.
Who can feed all these cattle?
The people who stay are crazy.
It would be better to burn our barns
to the ground and forget, leaving
the secrets inside unknowable.

3 January 12

Every day, another one dies.
Though our owners have returned,
though we no longer want for food or water,
the storm inside us hasn't been buried.
I feel it in me too—I can't explain
what's different now.
We never know who will go next.
We become afraid and religious.
How many more will die tomorrow?
Will I be next? I can't sleep at night,
I am wild with sex. I mount, I mount
becoming a mountain against
the back of a woman. For a moment,
I am eternal.

11 March 12

Three cows walk into a convenience store.
Some of them have begun to develop
white spots on their hides—
They wander in and out of houses
like ghosts on a pilgrimage—
It's better this way.
If they keep going, they might get
to the border of the radioactive zone.
By that point, someone will probably kill them.
But may they get farther. May they enter
a city that's alive, and even if they're shot down,
I hope a family sees them
with their strange white spots.
That a child asks her mother
where they got their spots.
That the child will look over the fence
that divides her life from the radioactive zone.
That she will wonder,
and it will be made known
all that we have done.

In Tokyo, three months after the earthquake,

everyone is living their lives normally,
everything is covered in stickers that say: Do <3 Japan.
The air-conditioning is off in every building,
saving for Tohoku, loving for Tohoku.
I drown in my sweat while that gaudy crab
looming over the seafood market
continues to move his giant claws up and down,
narcissist that he is.

Response to the Brother Who Wants to Move in After the Earthquake:

You are not welcome here.
You are contaminated.
You have radiation in your skin.
You breathed in that nuclear air.

You are contaminated;
a power plant lives in you now.
There's already radiation in your skin,
and I can't risk you rubbing off on me.

You carry that power plant inside you,
but we are genki here,
and I can't risk you rubbing off on us.
We want to live—

We are genki here, but
he who mixes with vermillion turns red.
I want to *live*,
I don't want to think about Fukushima.

Mixed with red ink, anything becomes red.
It can't be helped.
I don't want to think about Fukushima.
There are places for that sort of thing.

Shikata ga nai.
You breathed in that nuclear air.
There are places for that sort of thing, but
you are not welcome here.

exclusion zone ekphrasis

besides the dead bodies
in fields, this town

looks like any town,
like the disappeared people

might come back
at any minute:

the oranges on the table
still look ripe,

someone's left
their muddy boots at the door.

the radiation spirit
fills a room

with one big breath,
encasing a house

like a porcelain doll,
displayed but never touched—

who are we to look into
their windows with longing?

a couple comes
once a month in hazmat suits,

white like mourners, sweeping
the floor and sorting

through what's left. they bag
the trash and return

to their temporary home, waiting
for permission to return once more.

Animal Man

for Naoto Matsumura

I know what it feels like to be Adam:
to be the only man in a town
of animals, left to name them:

Miracle the Dog, Boss the Ostrich—
If the animals could name me,
what would I be called?

God said to Adam that man
is not meant to be alone,
but I find fellowship from the dogs

and pigs I free onto the streets.
They go in and out of houses,
wearing whatever falls on them.

Some days, they come out in old noren
partitions, suit jackets, schoolgirl dresses.
From a distance, I mistake them

for my missing neighbors:
Mr. Takei the burial man,
Mrs. Yamada at the onsen.

Only once they roll around in a muddy field
do my neighbors disappear,
replaced by animals.

Radium Girls

I. December 1923: Waterbury Clock Factory, Connecticut

my mouth is a room that lights up in the dark

the girl who trained me spatula-full of radium in her mouth corners of her lips gritty and glowing her reassurance that the paint was harmless taught us how to point the paintbrush tip between our lips

my manager says a little radon puts the sex in your cheeks nudging me

some girls hate the taste but i love it it tastes like eternity

no matter how many times i brush my teeth at night i taste that gritty glue

i'm good and quick i get more dials done than the other girls

sometimes i only get thirty dials done a day what will my mother say when she sees my paycheck

my mouth's been aching my mother blames my sweet tooth

last night a tooth came out i didn't have to do anything it just fell into my hand

other people buy radium soda radium candy radium facial creams but we get it for free we're the luckiest girls in the world

in the dark we are all suns our faces hands dresses glow like the dials we paint

one girl's halfway to becoming an angel her back all the way down to her waist glowing

soon we won't have to put it on at all it'll be in our bones it'll pour out from forever-twenty skin

II. August 2011: Miyakoji, Japan

when we visit our house we wear cough masks we wear suits

at our house the grass is tall and uncut everything is still on the floor where it fell when the earthquake hit

the body of a dog is tangled in our fence his body hasn't fully decomposed a patch of fur like a felt block remaining on his right ear

first thing: my father disposes of the dog my mother gets on her knees and begins scrubbing the floor in her gloves and suit she adjusts the family altar and burns a stick of incense

every time we go outside my father brings a meter on good days we can play on the blacktop for thirty minutes

my mother asks me if i feel alright if anything feels odd i think about stuffing my mouth with our flowers eating the expired candy in our kitchen and becoming my own power plant

on the edge of town a cleanup crew fills bags with radioactive waste there are lots of bags they fill up my old school's baseball field the bags get high enough to build a black wall

They say They'll get rid of the bags soon but my mother doesn't believe Them she says They are burying us inside our own waste because no one wants to look at us and feel guilty no one wants to remember what went wrong or change anything everyone wants to go back to work back to their homes and return to what they've always done

my mother's voice gets loud when she says this she's holding a watch her mother gave her when she was a girl like me she drops it and it falls to the floor the glass face cracks with one split sound even so it continues ticking my mother goes silent i am silent—it makes every tick seem louder than it really is

Operation Fantasia

*. . .by the end of 1944 . . . [the OSS] begun spraying live
foxes with luminous paint, hoping to release them across
the entire field of combat. . .*
—Greg Ross, *Futility Closet*

One by one, the foxes
    sink, but (relief!)
        come back up.

Paddling, they glow
    against the sea like
        festival lanterns.

A skulk of them plow
    in a line, the way a wedding party
        moves inside city.

Away from Japan, toward the Atlantic—
    a new horizon forms.
        No one wants to be at war.

Should they make it there,
    how will they be found:
        our mythological warfare?

Perhaps a priest will give a sutra,
    foxes running down the beach,
        wet like fresh laundry.

A neighbor might express concern
    about the sudden harvest loss
        for his azuki beans,

another reluctant to talk
    to strangers, afraid of accidently
        addressing a spirit.

A few years, & the foxes will be
    familiar, paint shed like old skin.
        All the while, a war continues.

It gets velvet dark,
      & the first one drowns.
           A heavy burden lifts from me.

What a sight our drowning moons
      must make—as if
           a sea-Hell were opened.

What might become
      of our enemies now,
           & all the more, of us?

Imagine future excavators, studying
      the ocean floor:
           & all those fox skulls, glowing.

原爆—Atom

how quickly
the body unfolds
like a paper crane,

unremembered
like a fish
in the silent sea
of floating fish:

black rain
leaves only a son's shadow
memorialized in a wall.

A girl remains
as only a name
in the stomach
of a Nagasaki lunchbox.

A woman's body
wears glass shards
like osteoderms,

still carrying the child
across a carbon-black world.
The child holds firmly
the woman's hand, even when

the maggots come,
even as she hungers, even
when this nuclear rapture

has removed her mother,
she holds.

Looking at an Abandoned Russian Theme Park
in Niigata, Japan

oh God of open windows,
God of new ruins,
God of all things green,
God of nine-year-old
festering dog food.
God of Russian peasant
dancer women, God of many
phones, God of outdated
computers, God of molded
woolly mammoth models,
God of broken matryoshka dolls,
who even feeds the sparrow.

*

廃虚の俳句 / modern ruins haiku

the bed is made / dishes in the sink / a burial in-progress

old pachinko faces / boxed in the attic / childhood's festival masks

brimming theme park closet / a Russian village of girls' / hand-sewn dresses

box of snake bones / intertwined / like nautical knots

polaroid face / so water damaged / more ghost than girl

greening washing machines / line the elementary school / waiting for class portraits

that single white dress / in the closet / farm house Havingsham

obedient ski boots / line the shelves / eager for feet

last week's snow / on the broken karaoke machine / an emptied village

imperial-god's dusty portrait / chrysanthemum-sealed / post-war trash

orphaned mansion crucifix / mary leaned over the bed / prayer for a punched-in wall

formaldehyde rat body / evaporates— / science's forgotten dentures

Hitora Hospital— / perhaps your greatest secret / is your true namesake

The Water Trade

In Japanese folklore, water has always been a pathway to the world of the dead.
                    —Manekute no Yurei, The Inviting Ghost Hand

The water trade, an occupation
my mother would never approve of—   muddy
like the river in my fishing town
where I sometimes played and came out   with my sleeves
stained. How many times I played
alone, now, a paid companion—

I prepare the men's baths, thinking about the way
my mother prepared baths for me   both of us
climbing into the hot water, our bare flesh touching—   funny:
how two people can touch that intimately,
yet step out of the steam and find themselves
two strangers inhabiting the same space.

And all of this is made in water:

at training, a girl taught me how to move my body
against a client's to create an orgasm without being entered.
A barrier is needed to make fantasy.
I realize this is why men like pornography:
there is always a barrier between them   and the woman
in the photo. Our job as women is to maintain the barrier.

The worst thing we can do, she told me.
is break him out of his dream.

She taught me how to prepare them.   *Prepare,*
as if dressing a corpse. I think about the women at the river
who washed bodies for burial when I lather
the soap on his back, his lower parts.   He moans.
We create excitement out of nothing,
we are god-like that way.

I continue a tradition of paid companionship
started by geishas, survived in my soaplands.
They used to call this the floating world, which it is:
the pleasure world. Not just the occupation here,
but I myself—I *am* a floating world. I am slowly floating away,
less and less remains of me.

To my customers, I am "Jean," I am Western,
sophisticated.   I get my first business card
and it carries the lie of me. I have dreams about Jean:
unlike me, she grips the men confidently, wanting

them. Sometimes, Jean plucks out my eyes,
tries to replace them with her own, but each time
they fall out like pebbles. In those dreams,
she asks me what I'm called
and I forget my own name.

How is it that I have been intimate
with so many men yet still don't know their names.

And how is it that I have had a man   dig
his fingers into my back with longing,
yet I still feel freshness in the memory
of my new stepfather, his imported family
turning me foreign. It's been years
since I ran away. No one has found me, let alone looked.

evaporated people

a fired man pretends to go to work,
his suit a performance,
until one day he never comes home.

midnight movers
remove the save file
of a person's life: human

erasure. it's easy to become
a ghost in a country of ghosts.
once upon a time a kappa

lures a boy into a nearby lake—
the body never found. last year,
a boy lured himself into a tide

of strangers, evaporated onto Bone Street.
a mother at home, left with
an empty room for an heir.

some villages still have signs near water:
be careful of kappas,
as if water is needed for a person to vanish.

Tsunami Debris Found Poem

After International Pacific Research Center's "Marine and Tsunami Debris Sightings"

date	picture	location	description
Before	[the ocean]	bellows: Oahu—!	After 3 days, vanished
First days of January,	[blue]	on Barking Sands.	Japan floated, then entered
Exact date unknown; found	[plastic]	island	capsized & adrift.
found	[a girl & a]	River mouth,	tongue and groove together.
late June	[buoys]	refuge	[for] camels & rhinos.
[four years after the tsunami]:	[several]	shipwrecks	found together, smelling of gasoline.
photo	[tires]	Kauai—Bike Path	says: Do not enter...authorized personnel only.
between	[ropes].	Lookout!	Gooseneck barnacles covered
the first week.	[Two men]	floated eight miles off, then lost to sight.	Fragment of
and	[ship bumper],	sacred	debris. Confirmed
[the] same	[Pleasure boat]	floated off Life.	Not interested in having it back.

Clean-up Crew

Hanauma Bay, Oahu

Cleaning up the beach reminds me
of cleaning my room, only now
my room is the ocean
& everyday someone comes in
& pours trash in my bed
so that I'm sleeping on filth.

Today, I found a refrigerator
that reminds me
of my grandmother:
up to my waist, rust-orange body,
all hollowed out.

I know this refrigerator belonged
to someone, that it is missed,
but each day the beaches
are so covered that even after
a full day there are piles, dark
with unnamed things.

Minamisanriku, Japan

Now with all the buildings gone
you can see the mountain again—
the base covered in debris
like a bedroom floor,
a disassembled toy city left
to be cleaned up. Where
to begin? One man in the middle
of what once was a road
sweeps, reveals
a white and peeling dividing line.

Burusera

Beside his bed, the salary man keeps
a collection of pink panties,
bows and glitter on the elastic band.

Sniffing the crotch, he imagines
what living thing is building
inside her, like an orchestra,

like a surging forest. He
knows this. Certainly, holding the fabric,
her scent begins to grow in him

as well—first in the nose, a flower.
Then the cavity of his mouth. It thickens
on the back of his tongue until

small trees begin to come out of
his ears, a deer inhabits his left
tear duct. He cries, and the deer

leaps down the river of his cheek.
I have never been so full, he says over
and over, receding and returning like a tide.

A String of Buoys Arrive on Oahu Beach

The people in Japan want Americans to know that none of the
debris is garbage. To them, many of those items are sacred.
—Gary Horcher, October 12, 2012

we arrived on the beach Christmas morning, tangled together
    like babes in umbilical cords

we arrived on the beach with barnacle-mouths, covered like lepers,
    knowing our season of use had long passed

hopeful that someone might find us, we waited

we dwelled with the crates & a rusted propane tank, strangers
    who also were lost in the years of the storm

each morning the tank spat out pieces of home, stinking
    like old market fish

it took us three years to arrive, two weeks to be found

some of us thought they might make us into a display
    to remember disaster—

as if in our service, we morphed into holy tool gods

some of us already missed the familiar sea, ready to sit at our posts

some of us worried as strangers collected us, tossing our bodies
    to dumpsters with wide eager mouths

Okinawa Aquarium

Framed & mounted on the wall, a dolphin's stomach, splayed.
Inside: plastic bags, bottle caps, condoms, broken
coke bottles, tampons, lighters, dentures, toys and bubble
wands. If God cut me open with a scalpel, what

would He find inside me? My beached body,
heavy with human gospel. Removing each piece from me,
God would say: *I gave you so many trees to eat from.*
I might say: *I felt so full—even briefly, I thought I was really filled.*

Tokyo Steakhouse

i.

I wanted a Japanese man to love me, but when the businessman—
his voice slurred with sake—told me I was pretty, I did not
desire. He was not my manga hero. He was sweating loneliness,
and, though younger than my father, his hair was hinting gray.

I was fourteen years old. He asked me what I did—and being
the kind of girl who wanted to do something, I told him I was
a writer, a poet—

He looked at me with blank wet fish eyes, and not knowing how
to translate these things I said, *Haiku! A person who does haiku.*

He nodded, and we came to a truce.

*

My father turned to him and asked how his wife was doing,

he said, *I do not know.*

My mother and I think about that wife sometimes.

ii.

We met the secretary at the restaurant. In her pink suit, she laughed in her hand at all the right parts. She said nothing the whole night.

The qi pao silk against my thighs—Chinese elegance—seemed wise at the time. In my seat I felt like a stranger against the sea of suits.

Our cook grilled on a wheeled steel grill beside my mother while she thumbed the Book of John on her lap, knowing there is only so much time.

But all I could focus on were the songs of waitresses singing Happy Birthday to every table, their textbook English ornamental:

and many more. . .

and I thought about how
somewhere—this moment—
someone is being born.

Baptism

Fukuoka, Summer 2011

Our suited pastor,
standing in the ocean,

water dark up to his thighs.
From the shore, he looks

like a lone oyster buoy,
returning from a storm.

Kaylee beside him,
an American skyscraper.

Behind them, a still horizon, blue.
Strange, this water: the same

that buried five cities, now
over Kaylee's shoulders,

a celebration. From the shore,
we, the church, stand holding

our shoes, feet bare
in the sand, waiting. Out east,

new cities will be built.
Inside Kaylee, a renovated

city is filling.
She rises from the water.

*

Notes

Remember the calamity of the great tsunamis. Do not build any homes below this point.
                    —Aneyoshi tsunami stone

"Onagawa," pg. 4

Inspired by the footage "2011 Japan Tsunami: Onagawa [stabilized with Deshaker]," YouTube video, 2:59, John9612, Mar 11, 2013.

"Town Hall," pg. 7

From *The New York Times*' article "Tsunami Warnings, Written in Stone" (2011): "One idea, put forth by a group of researchers, calls for preserving some of the buildings ruined by the recent tsunami to serve as permanent reminders of the waves' destructive power, much as the skeletal Atomic Bomb Dome in Hiroshima warns against nuclear war.

"'We need a modern version of the tsunami stones,' said Masayuki Oishi, a geologist at the Iwate Prefectural Museum in Morioka."

For more information on tsunami stones, visit *Smithsonian Magazine*'s article "These Century-Old Stone "Tsunami Stones" Dot Japan's Coastline" (2015).

"Rumiko / A Series of Possessions," pg. 8

Inspired by Richard Lloyd Parry's article in *London Review of Books* "Ghosts of the Tsunami."

"Mizuko," pg. 12

Mizuko (水子) literally "water child," is a Japanese term for a stillborn baby. (Wikipedia)

For further reading, visit *NPR*'s article "Adopting A Buddhist Ritual To Mourn Miscarriage, Abortion" (2015).

"Corpse Washing," pg. 14

Inspired by the 2008 film *Departures* (おくりびと).

"Tsunami Girl," pg. 16

The term "fox's wedding" can mean a range of things, depending on regional traditions. It is typically used to reference rain on a sunny day, but its connotation as an ill omen gesturing toward a looming death or a funeral ritual is lore specific to the Tokushima region. For more information, visit: https://japanesemythology.wordpress.com/tag/kitsune-no-yomeiri/

"NASA Satellite Triolet," pg. 23

Inspired by NASA Earth Observatory images, captured on March 14th 2011, showing the severe flooding of the Kitakami River three days after the earthquake. To view these images, visit NASA's earth observatory online.

"Coming Home after a Tsunami," pg. 24

Shuntaro Tanikawa is a legendary poet in Japan who also translates the *Peanuts* comic strip into Japanese. I highly encourage readers unfamiliar with his work to take a look. There are many fantastic translations of his work in English. His magical realism sensibilities combined with a good sense of humor and accessibility leave incredible, fantastical images lingering even after reading.

"Poem for the Sneakers Washing Onshore," pg. 25

Inspired by KHQ's article "'We're Expecting 100 Sneakers With Bones In Them'" (2012).

"Villanelle from an Okawa School Mother," pg. 26

Inspired by *Telegraph*'s article "Mother excavates tsunami-hit school to find daughter's body."

"Ningyo Kuyo (Doll Funeral Ceremony)," pg. 28

人形供養 (ningyo kuyo) is a ritual to dispose of unwanted dolls. Because superstition dictates that dolls have spirits, they must be brought to a local jinjya (temple) for a priest to give the doll last rites.

"Fukushima Syndrome," pg. 32

From Cleanenergy.org's blog post "Japan Continues Struggle with Aftermath from the Fukushima Nuclear Disaster" (2012): "This fall, an illness dubbed the 'Fukushima syndrome' was reported to be killing cattle near the Fukushima prefecture."

"Animal Man," pg. 39

For more information on Naoto Matsumura, check out the *Washington Post* article "Caring for Fukushima's abandoned animals" (2016).

"Radium Girls," pg. 40

 Inspired by Bored Panda's images in the post "Never-Before-Seen Images Reveal How The Fukushima Exclusion Zone Was Swallowed By Nature."

For further reading, visit Kate Moore's *The Radium Girls: The Dark Story of America's Shining Women* (2017).

"原爆 —Atom," pg. 44

Inspired by the 2016 film *In This Corner of the World* (この世界の片隅に).

原爆 (genbaku) refers to the atomic bomb. The Genbaku dome is part of the Hiroshima peace memorial, remains in its state of ruin from the atomic bomb drop in 1945.

This poem was also inspired by my visit to the Hiroshima Peace Memorial Museum in 2011. To see some of the exhibits, feel free to visit the exhibits on their website: http://hpmmuseum.jp.

"Looking at an Abandoned Russian Themepark in Niigata, Japan," pg. 45

I encourage readers to view the images urban explorers have taken of the abandoned Niigata Russian Village. Tokyo Times, Michael John Grist, and Abandoned Kansai have some incredible images as well as additional background on the unusual park.

"廃虚の俳句 / modern ruins haiku," pg. 47

Haikyo (**廃虚**) in Japanese means "obsolete hill," and is used in reference to ruins, particularly contemporary ruins. It also is in reference to urban exploration, the act of visiting contemporary ruins. Due to the 80s economic boom and subsequent crash in the 90s/early 2000s, as well as Japan's complex property ownership laws, *haikyo* are a particularly common phenomena in Japan.

"evaporated people," pg. 50

For further reading, check out Léna Mauger's *The Vanished: The "Evaporated People" of Japan in Stories and Photographs* (2016) and *New York Post*'s article "The Chilling Stories Behind Japan's 'Evaporating People'" (2016).

"Tsunami Debris Found Poem," pg. 51

Inspired by the *International Pacific Research Center*'s Marine and Tsunami Debris Sightings chart, which can be viewed online at their site: http://iprc.soest.hawaii.edu. For more information about the tsunami debris, visit BBC's article "Japan's tsunami debris: Five remarkable stories" (2016).

"Burusera," pg. 53

When I learned about the burusera addiction, I tried to understand what the appeal was—and why grown men would find hope and arousal in children's clothing. So I wrote a poem. When I don't understand something, when I think something is inhuman or bizarre, I try to write a poem so I can inhabit that perspective briefly—and though I may still find the practice disturbing, I can understand the humanness that invokes and abides in that experience. The word orchestra became a critical turning point for me, as I thought of the Japanese word karaoke, which literally means "empty orchestra." An orchestra is filled when a voice is added. We are all trying to fill a certain emptiness in us. How we choose to provide that voice for fullness varies.

Additional Resources

花は咲く(NHK World's "Flowers Will Bloom," a song in memory of 3/11)

Svetlana Alexievich's *Voices from Chernobyl: The Oral History of a Nuclear Disaster* (1997)

David Lochbaum's *Fukushima: The Story of a Nuclear Disaster* (2014)

David McNeill's *Strong in the Rain: Surviving Japan's Earthquake, Tsunami, and Fukushima Nuclear Disaster* (2012)

April Naoko Heck's poetry collection *A Nuclear Family* (2014)

Lee Ann Roripaugh's poetry collection *Tsunami vs the Fukushima 50* (2019)

Kathleen Burkinshaw's kidlit novel *The Last Cherry Blossom* (2016)

This American Life's episode "Really Long Distance"

The United Nation's Disarmament educational resources: https://www.un.org/disarmament/education/teachers-students.html

Physicians for Social Responsibility's resource page: https://www.psr.org/resources/?_sft_resource_category=nuclear-power

On the state of Fukushima today:

The Diplomat's article "The Truth About Radiation in Fukushima" (2019)

Quartz's article "The UN says Japan may be violating human rights by returning families to Fukushima" (2018)

Acknowledgments

To God be the glory, great things He has done.

To Jenn Givhan, for giving thoughtful, honest feedback on earlier drafts of this manuscript, and for your constant encouragement through this writing journey. I feel honored to call you a friend. This book wouldn't be here without you.

To Collegeville and The Glen for phenomenal workshops and some much needed time to sit with these poems. To Michael Dennis Browne and Carolyn Forche and all the amazing and gifted writers in my cohorts, thank you. These poems wouldn't be here without you.

To Sally Rosen Kindred for all our Panera Bread write-ins and the encouragement to keep persisting, especially through the submission process. Thank you for believing in this book and your confidence that it would find the right home in time.

To Chris Kondrich, Hiram Larew, Laura Shovan, Queen Alike, Johnna Schmidt, Aaron Brown and Marlena Chertock for encouragement and fellowship through this bizarre and beautiful journey called poetry.

Thank you, Pamela Winters, for your valuable feedback and fellowship. Your encouragement toward these poems kept me going through the tide of rejection letters.

Thank you, Kathleen Burkinshaw, for all your amazing informational resources on abolishing nuclear weapons and spreading peace.

Thank you to Christopher Forrest for believing in these poems and spending so much thoughtful time with them. You have gone above and beyond the call of duty and have helped me see these poems on a deeper level. I will be forever grateful. Thank you, Kevin Morgan Watson, and Press 53 for giving this manuscript a lovely home.

To Brandy Whitlock and Dr. Susan Cohen for believing in me and my work. I don't know if I would have remained on this path without your feedback and encouragement.

I am forever indebted to the faculty at University of Maryland's MFA program who pushed me to do better as a poet. Thank you Josh Weiner, Liz Arnold and Michael Collier. I would not be the writer and instructor I am now without you.

In memory of Stan Plumly. Thank you for always pushing me to do better and teaching me to never settle for a mediocre poem. You are greatly missed.

In memory of all those who were and still are affected by 3/11, the Great East Japan Earthquake and tsunami, Fukushima powerplant disaster. You are not forgotten.

Meg Eden's work is published or forthcoming in magazines including *Prairie Schooner, Poetry Northwest, Crab Orchard Review, RHINO* and *CV2*. She teaches creative writing at Anne Arundel Community College and the MA program at Southern New Hampshire University. She is the author of five poetry chapbooks and the novel *Post-High School Reality Quest* (2017). She runs the Magfest MAGES Library blog, which posts accessible academic articles about video games. Find her online at www.megedenbooks.com or on Twitter at @ConfusedNarwhal.

CPSIA information can be obtained
at www.ICGtesting.com
Printed in the USA
BVHW032334060120
568774BV00001B/11/P